GREAT
MOTORCYCLES

GREAT
MOTORCYCLES

AN EXHILARATING COLLECTION OF THE GREATEST MOTORCYCLES

PaRragon

Bath · New York · Singapore · Hong Kong · Cologne · Delhi
Melbourne · Amsterdam · Johannesburg · Auckland · Shenzhen

First published by Parragon in 2011

Parragon
Queen Street House
4 Queen Street
Bath BA1 1HE, UK

Designed, produced, and packaged by
Stonecastle Graphics Limited

Designed by Sue Pressley and Paul Turner
Text by Philip de Ste. Croix

ISBN 978-1-4454-2889-5

Printed in China

Page one: *Larry Pegram wins on a Ducati in the 2009 AMA*
Superbike Championship round at Topeka Park, Kansas.

Page two: *Kawasaki's VN1700 Classic tourer in its element.*

Page three: *Indian Motorcycle Company—an American great.*

Right: *Choppers are custom bikes that are either modified*
production machines or exotic creations built from scratch.

Contents

Introduction

The raw appeal of being astride a powerful motorcycle comes from a combination of many sensations: satisfaction at being in control of a piece of hi-tech engineering, a sense of freedom, exposure to the elements, and a hint of danger, not to mention the electric thrill of acceleration possible on a machine with a power-to-weight ratio that other road users can only dream about.

That underlying sense of excitement was experienced by riders 100 years ago in the early days of motorcycling, and it remains a potent force today for those who ride simply for fun or to escape from the pressures of the modern world. In that time the bikes themselves have evolved from simple single-cylinder machines to ultra-sophisticated devices capable of almost 200 mph (322 kph). Yet the feeling that comes from gripping a pair of handlebars and winding the throttle back to its stop remains much the same.

This book aims to convey some of the sense of excitement that comes from being around great motorcycles. It picks up the story in the middle of the last century when Harley-Davidson was striding clear of the competition in the United States, while manufacturers in Great Britain, Germany, and Italy ruled the roost in Europe.

The second section takes the story into the twenty-first century, with the rise of the Japanese giants and the amazing period of engineering cross-fertilization that saw race-bred technology feed through into a range of awesome road-going superbikes. It also reviews the current line-up of top bikes from compact middleweights to mighty tourers and cruisers that rumble along the world's freeways, and the mind-blowingly fast superbikes that leave all trailing in their wake.

In the final section attention turns to the track—both the paved circuits used for top-level road racing and the rugged dirt terrain that is the territory beloved of motocross, enduro, and speedway riders. It provides a fittingly adrenaline-fueled conclusion to this wonderfully illustrated tribute to the world's great motorcycles.

Right: Harley-Davidson has led the way in the factory custom segment of the market since the days of the FX Super Glide. The 2010 model XL1200 Sportster Custom offers a low custom tank, low-rise handlebars, and a bullet headlamp.

A World of Classics

Below: Ariel's Red Hunter is fondly remembered as one of the most dependable motorcycles of the 1950s, and this Red Hunter 350 dating from 1956 was a characteristically solid and reliable machine, powered by a slow-revving 18 bhp pushrod engine, which sent it rumbling along to a top speed of just over 70 mph (113 kph). It was popular with riders impressed by the competitive price, good fuel economy, decent handling, and excellent finish.

Left: The Benelli marque was founded in 1911 by the Benelli brothers, but its fortunes were in decline when it was bought by Alessandro de Tomaso in 1972. The revamped range included the Tornado 650S—a 643 cc parallel twin that pulled happily and strongly from low revs.

Opposite: The 1952-model Ariel Square Four, nicknamed the "Squariel," was a stylish bike whose flexible 997 cc four-cylinder engine justified the company's advertising boast of "Ten to a hundred in top gear." The engine was heavily finned in an effort to cool the rear cylinders.

Opposite: One of the most glamorous of the pre-World War II roadsters, the Brough Superior was advertised as "the Rolls-Royce of motorcycles." This is the 990 cc side-valve SS80 model. Its bigger brother, the SS100, was an impressive, high-performance 988 cc V-twin capable of a top speed of 100 mph (161 kph). The most famous owner of one of these exclusive machines was T. E. Lawrence (Lawrence of Arabia) and he wrote of it, "It is the silkiest thing I have ever ridden…I think it is going to be a very excellent bike."

Left: BMW was the major supplier of motorcycles to the German Wehrmacht during World War II. The R75 was a 745 cc sidecar unit that was intended for cross-country use. Production began in 1941 and almost 18,000 machines had been delivered to the army by 1944.

Below: A 1959 BMW R50 pictured in a beautiful Alpine setting. This model was one of a new range of BMW motorcycles with Earles forks and enclosed drive shafts. The engine was a four-stroke two-cylinder 494 cc flat twin, and top speed was around 87 mph (140 kph).

Above: This racing bike won the 1972 Imola 200-mile (332-km) race. It is a Ducati 750 Imola Desmo, designed by Fabio Taglioni and was ridden by Paul Smart. Teammate Bruno Spaggiari followed him home in second place. It proved a historic victory for Ducati and generated very positive publicity.

Right: The lean, racy BSA Gold Star Clubman was the ultimate street-legal competition bike of the 1950s. Capable of 110 mph (177 kph), the classic Gold Star look included chrome-flanked fuel tank, big front drum brake, heavily finned single-cylinder motor, and swept-back exhaust.

Opposite: The key ingredients for a successful bike in the United States in the mid-1950s were style, performance, and engine capacity. BSA's powerful and good-looking 650 cc Road Rocket, launched in the States in 1954, had plenty of all three, and it sold well in this all-important market.

Left: Harley-Davidson's 1958-model Duo-Glide was a landmark motorcycle. As the telescopic front forks and chrome-encased rear shocks proclaimed for all to see, this bike had suspension at both ends rather than just up front, as had been the case up until then.

Opposite: An Indian Chief of 1940s' or early 1950s' vintage, with its big V-twin engine complemented by the enormous and curvaceous front fenders, is one of the most instantly recognizable motorcycles ever produced. Unfortunately the market was just too tough and Indian shut down in 1953.

Above: The WL45 was a smaller cousin of Harley-Davidson's stable of large-capacity V-twins. The Forty-Five had a 750 cc side-valve engine. It produced only 25 bhp but performance was robust, and the bike proved popular during the 1930s and 1940s. It also saw extensive military service with the US Army during World War II as the WLA.

Left: The Indian Four was stylish, comfortable, fast, and expensive. It featured an in-line four-cylinder 1,265 cc engine. It remained in production for 15 years between the late 1920s and the early 1940s and was progressively updated over that period. This is a late Four distinguished by its impressive skirted fenders and rear plunger suspension.

Left: Launched in 1968, one of the most famous and best-loved of British bikes, the Norton Commando used innovative rubber chassis mountings to reduce engine vibration.

Opposite: The 500 cc parallel-twin Dominator Model 7 was Norton's answer to Triumph's revolutionary Speed Twin. This 1952 example has the popular chromed headlamp peak.

Below: Moto Guzzi's 498 cc single-cylinder Falcone remained in production for 18 years during the 1950s and 1960s. This is a 1964 Turismo version.

Left: *The Sunbeam S8, introduced in 1949, was essentially a sportier and more reliable version of the S7, which had sold poorly following its release two years earlier. The S8 featured a smooth and reliable 487 cc tandem-twin engine.*

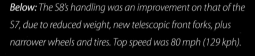

Below: *The S8's handling was an improvement on that of the S7, due to reduced weight, new telescopic front forks, plus narrower wheels and tires. Top speed was 80 mph (129 kph).*

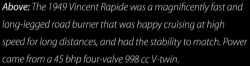

Above: *The 1949 Vincent Rapide was a magnificently fast and long-legged road burner that was happy cruising at high speed for long distances, and had the stability to match. Power came from a 45 bhp four-valve 998 cc V-twin.*

Opposite: *Vincent's thundering V-twins were the world's fastest and finest roadsters in the1940s and early 1950s, combining exhilarating high performance with stable handling, excellent braking, and long-distance cruising ability. This Series C Rapide, produced in 1950, featured Vincent's Girdraulic front forks instead of the previous Series B model's Brampton girders.*

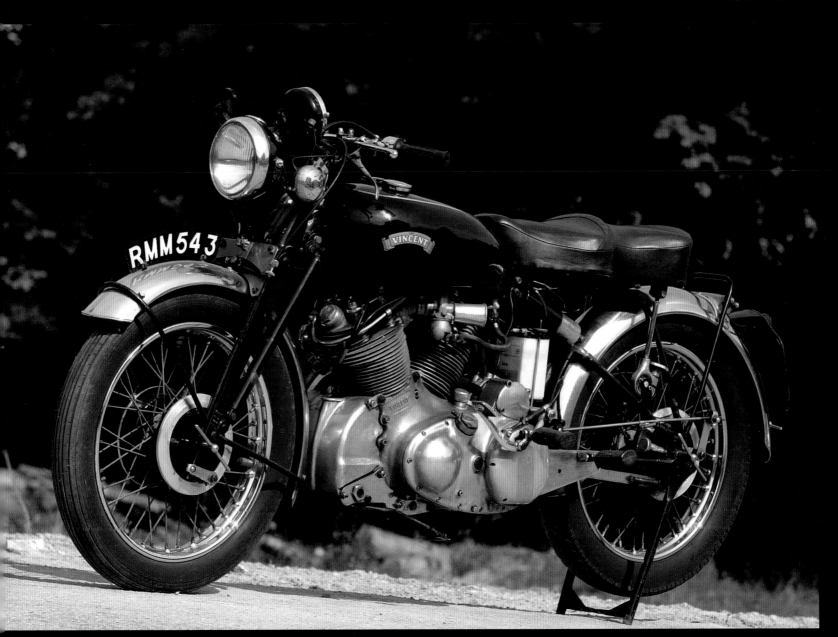

Above: Triumph created its most famous and popular model—the Bonneville—in 1959 by fitting the existing 649 cc Tiger 110 with a new cylinder head and twin carburetors. The resulting sports roadster was named Bonneville after the famous salt flats in Utah where a streamlined Triumph had set a speed record of 214 mph (344 kph) in 1956. Its lean lines and rev-happy engine made it one of the most popular bikes on the road during the 1960s.

Right: Triumph's Tiger 100 was a hotted-up version of the revolutionary Speed Twin. It was one of the fastest bikes around in the late 1940s and early 1950s. The pulled-back handlebars allowed the rider to crouch over the tank in order to make the most of its near 100 mph (161 kph) top speed.

Opposite: The Triumph Thunderbird became the epitome of cool when it was ridden by Marlon Brando in the 1953 film The Wild One. It was a strikingly lean and stylish machine and the smooth and reliable 649 cc parallel-twin engine was good for performance touching on the "ton" (100 mph/161 kph).

Power and Performance

Right: Aprilia's RSV4R is a technology-packed, beautifully balanced Italian superbike. At its heart is a liquid-cooled 998 cc V4 motor that produces a claimed 180 bhp, and accelerates the bike to a top speed of 180 mph (290 kph). It has a six-speed cassette gearbox as well as a ride-by-wire throttle system.

Above: The racing version of Aprilia's RSV4R was a success in its first year of competition in the 2009 World Superbike Championship. Factory rider Max Biaggi came fourth in the rankings. For 2010 it wore a Tricolor livery representing the team's partnership with the Alitalia airline.

Left: Aprilia's 850 cc Mana GT sprung quite a surprise when it was launched in 2009—it does not have a gearbox. Instead it uses a CVT (continuously variable transmission), which means that you can ride it like a scooter without the need to change gear—just twist the throttle and away you go!

Left: This awe-inspiring creation is the 2008 Benelli TNT Café 1130 Racer. It is powered by an 1,130 cc in-line triple. A crafty button on the dash allows the engine control unit to be switched between free power and controlled power for better control of the bike in poor traction conditions.

Below: Motorcycles that spring from a racing heritage have to be both powerful and light. Benelli's TNT 1300 Titanium achieves lightness through the use of modern manufacturing materials such as aluminum, carbon, titanium, and a lightweight alloy called ergal used in the rear shocks.

Above and Top: Shown in "naked" (top) and fully faired form (above), the Benelli Tornado Tre 1130 model that was first unveiled in 2006 signaled the ambition of this relatively small Italian manufacturer to position itself alongside the likes of Aprilia and Ducati as a force to be reckoned with in the supersports bike category. Featuring aggressive styling, the Tornado was powered by an 1,130 cc in-line triple that developed 120 kW at 10,500 rpm.

Above: *The Italian firm of Bimota was founded in 1972 to build bespoke sports bikes based around other manufacturers' engines. The SB1 used a 500 cc Suzuki engine and was manufactured between 1975 and 1977. The machine dominated the Italian junior national championships, taking the title five times between 1976 and 1980.*

Left: *The DB4ie comes later in Bimota's racing history. This Ducati-engined machine dates from 2000 and it used the 900 SS V-twin powerplant. The ie designation referred to the electronic fuel injection system that superseded the carburetors that had been fitted to the original DB4.*

Opposite: *Bimota's YB2 also dates from the late 1970s, but in this case the power was supplied by a 250 cc Yamaha in-line twin. The YB2 won four times during the 1976 world championship season, Otello Buscherini taking the 350 class Grand Prix on one at Imola in that year.*

Right: Concept 6 was first unveiled by BMW at the 2009 Milan Motorcycle Show in Italy. It featured a huge 1,650 cc in-line straight-six engine mounted transversely across the chassis. This technology found its way into the new K1600 touring bikes that were announced in 2010.

Above: BMW's R1200GS Adventure is the latest member of a family of dual-sport (street-legal bikes designed for both on- and off-road use) motorcycles that have been in production since 1981. This bike uses a 1,170 cc horizontally opposed flat-twin (boxer) engine and shaft drive.

Right: In the 1990s the term "naked" became a popular way to describe street bikes that dispensed with fairings and windshields to flaunt their aggressive lines unashamedly. BMW's naked contender is the K1300R, which the company's website trumpets as "the coolest power in town."

Opposite: BMW initially built the S1000RR sport bike to compete in the 2009 Superbike World Championship, but then expanded production in 2010 to offer it for sale commercially. It is powered by a 999 cc in-line four through a six-speed gearbox, and top speed is over 124 mph (200 kph).

Above: Boss Hoss builds big bikes! The company was founded by Monte Warne in 1990 and is based in Dyersburg, Tennessee. It manufactures motorcycles and trikes equipped with V8 engines, produced by General Motors, and semi-automatic transmissions. This is a BHC-3 502 from 2007.

Above: The BHC-3 ZZ4 from Boss Hoss uses a massive 5,700 cc (that's 350 cubic inches) liquid-cooled V8 engine that is mounted longitudinally in the frame. These are the super-heavyweights of the bike world—the dry weight of a ZZ4 is more than 1,110 lb (500 kg), around half a ton!

Left: This is the Supersport or SS version of the Boss Hoss ZZ4. Although these are very large and rather dauntingly heavy machines, they are surprisingly easy and fun to ride. The engine features an automatic transmission, which does away with the need for manual gear changes.

Above: The 2010 Indian Chief Bomber was produced as a limited edition model that would only be offered for one year. The two finishes illustrated were warrior green smoke and silver smoke. The tank featured a hand-painted pin-up reminiscent of the mascots that adorned WW II American bombers.

Above: Indian motorcycle company's fortunes went into decline after World War II and production ended in 1953. However, the name was revived in 2006 and the production lines started rolling again in 2008. This is a 2010 Indian Chief Vintage, which uses a 1,720 cc Powerplus V-twin engine.

Right: The Buell 1125R superbike is manufactured by Buell Motorcycle Company in the United States and was introduced in 2007 for the 2008 model year. It is powered by a 1,125 cc Helicon liquid-cooled V-twin engine produced by Rotax of Austria. Drive is by belt rather than chain.

Above: MV Agusta's 2010 model of the 1090 RR Brutale features a split dial with a rev counter and two multifunction LCD screens providing a wide variety of data.

Left: The F4 was the motorcycle that announced MV Agusta's dramatic rebirth in the 1990s. The 2010 model continued the quest for motorcycle excellence.

Opposite: The original MV Agusta Brutale was created by Massimo Tamburini, the designer of the Ducati 916. The 1090 RR model featured a larger 1,078 cc engine.

Left: Over the years from its introduction in 1971, Moto Guzzi's California tourer saw several restyles and revisions, notably in its engine capacity which grew to 850, 950, and finally 1,100cc. The distinctive V-twin is mounted across the frame. This California III dates from 2007.

Right: Cagiva made a high-profile debut as a superbike manufacturer with the Raptor and V-Raptor, a pair of eye-catching machines powered by the TL1000 V-twin from Suzuki. The bikes were seriously quick with superb handling characteristics. Pictured here is a 2005 Raptor 1000.

Above: The Ducati Desmosedici RR is a limited production road-legal version of the Desmosedici MotoGP racebike. It is powered by a 989 cc desmodromic-valve V4 engine.

Opposite: The 2005-vintage Ducati Supersport 1000DS (for dual spark) used an advanced tubular steel trellis frame and superior suspension to ensure excellent handling.

Below: The Ducati Paul Smart 1000LE was built by Ducati in 2006 to commemorate Smart's victory at the Imola 200 race in 1972, a win that helped to define Ducati's racing future.

Above: Characterized by aggressive looks and a naked frame, the Monster series of Ducati bikes was first unveiled by the company in the early 1990s. They have been hugely successful commercially accounting for a large proportion of worldwide sales. This is a 2006 Monster 695 model.

Right: Designed by Fabio Taglioni, the Pantah 500 is where the current line of Ducati V-twins began. First shown in December 1979, it was the Pantah's air-cooled 499 cc V-twin engine, with belt drive to single overhead camshafts, that signaled a new era in Ducati's history and a revival of its fortunes.

Above: Harley-Davidson bikes are guaranteed to catch the eye with modern styling that nevertheless contains visual references looking back to the company's history. This is a current generation Softail, the FXCWC Rocker C. Naturally the engine is a V-twin—a 1,584 cc air-cooled twin-cam unit.

Left: Harley's Heritage Softail Classic very intentionally echoes an earlier era—that of the famous 1950s Duo-Glide. With its spoked wheels, whitewall tires, retro-style fenders, and leather saddlebags, the styling looks back half a century, but the underlying technology is right up-to-date.

Opposite: Harley introduced its Road King range of tourers in the mid-1990s and they have remained in the line-up ever since. The innovative Touring chassis is based on a single-spar, rigid backbone frame and a stout swingarm developed to withstand the demands of long-haul touring riders.

Above: *The Harley-Davidson Dyna family has its roots in the factory-custom revolution of the 1970s and the seminal FX Super Glide that appeared in 1971. It combines Big Twin performance with an extended FX front end. This view of a 2010 FXDF Dyna Fat Bob emphasizes the bobtail rear fender.*

Below: *Designed by the celebrated Willie G. Davidson, the Fat Boy first made an appearance in the Harley-Davidson range in 1990. The fantastic retro styling and solid disc front wheel proved an instant crowd-pleaser. For 2010 the Fat Boy got the blacked-out treatment and lowered suspension.*

Above: *The V-Rod that Harley-Davidson unveiled in mid-2000 was a stunningly stylish, original, and powerful machine. This is the 2010 version—the VRSCF V-Rod Muscle.*

Opposite: *The first Harley Dyna Wide Glide appeared in 1993 with distinctive chopper style, kicked out, wide-set front fork legs, and subsequent models maintain the theme.*

Right: *Harley's Electra Glide Ultra Limited tourer takes its styling cues from the famous Electra Glide of 1965. It is equipped with a large handlebar-mounted fairing and windshield.*

Above: Honda's Goldwing range of touring motorcycles stretches all the way back to 1975 and the original GL1000, but the twenty-first-century versions set new standards for performance and comfort. This 2006 GL1800A Goldwing was powered by a fuel-injected 1,832 cc six-cylinder engine.

Below: A 2006-model Honda ST1300 sport touring motorcycle. Superseding the ST1100, the bike featured a 1,260 cc liquid-cooled V4 engine mounted as a stressed member in a light aluminum frame, five-speed shaft drive, and a fully-faired body with standard hard panniers.

Above: The Honda CBR600RR is a 599 cc supersport motorcycle that was introduced in 2003 as a race replica version of Honda's all-conquering MotoGP racebikes.

Opposite: The CBR1000RR that Honda unleashed in 2004 was one of the most outrageous models to grace the hugely successful Fireblade line. This is a 2008 model Fireblade.

Right: Honda updated the popular middleweight CB600F Hornet for 2009 with new adjustable suspension and styling updates including black metallic parts and new colors.

Opposite: Kawasaki advertised its new flagship tourer for 2010, the 1400GTR, as one of the most hi-tech sport tourers on the market. It featured traction control, ABS braking, and multi-function instrument displays. Power came from a 1,352 cc in-line four with variable valve timing.

Right: Kawasaki's Ninja 250R has the looks and style of a full-blown Ninja but is designed for easy handling, allowing riders new to motorcycling to experience the fun of a bike with supersports looks on an entry-level machine. At its heart is a 249 cc liquid-cooled parallel-twin engine.

Above: When the Kawasaki ZZ-R1100 was launched in 1990, the level of performance put it far ahead of the opposition. It remained the world's fastest bike for the next five years. Twenty years later, this is latest version—the ZZR1400. Its 1,352 cc in-line four develops 200 bhp.

Left: Kawasaki's range of Ninja motorcycles dates back to the mid 1980s and the launch of the ground-breaking GPZ900R, which set new standards for unbeatable four-cylinder performance. The 2010 Ninja ZX-10R maintains the tradition; searing power comes from a 998 cc in-line four.

Left: Suzuki's Boulevard M109R cruiser was introduced in 2006. The 109 designation referred to the size of the fuel-injected V-twin engine—109 cubic inches or 1,783 cc. The engine benefited from a shot of the race-proven technology developed for the championship-winning GSX-R sport bikes.

Above: The C90T touring variant of the Suzuki Boulevard has an aerodynamic windshield and a custom-designed backrest, suitable for comfortable long-range cruising on the open freeway. The engine is the 90 cubic inch (1,482 cc) version of the air-cooled ohc 45-degree V-twin.

Left: The M90 Boulevard draws its inspiration from the mighty M109 cruiser. The styling is modern and streamlined, with a sporty front fender that complements the smooth, tapered headlight cowl, cast aluminum alloy wheels, dual chromed exhausts, and chromed drag-style handlebars.

Opposite: Suzuki offered the Boulevard (sold in Europe as the Intruder) in two styles—M and C series. M models sported a more aggressive muscular look, while C's had classic cruiser lines (C109R shown right). The numbers in the model code described the engine capacity in cubic inches.

Left: Suzuki's original GSX-R750 became the first modern race replica production bike on its release in 1985. This was followed in 1997 by a smaller version—the 599 cc GSX-R600. It instantly became the sportiest middleweight on the market. And so it remains in its latest guise today.

Above: When Suzuki first launched the GSX1300R Hayabusa in 1999, the intention was plain—this was to be the fastest roadbike in the world, faster than Honda's Super Blackbird. And so it proved with a top speed of 190 mph (306 kph). Ten years on and the Hayabusa name is still globally renowned as a benchmark of high-performance bikes.

Left: The GSX-R1000 burst onto the scene at the start of the new millennium with a devastating combination of speed and agility. Suzuki did not rest on its laurels, however; revised models continue to keep the GSX-R at the front of the pack.

Opposite: With its drooping nose, large front fender, and bulky tail, the Hayabusa was not the most attractive superbike on the market, but it remains a huge success. Suzuki's engineers spent hours in the wind tunnel fine-tuning the design to guarantee superb aerodynamic efficiency.

Above: The T595 Daytona was the bike with which Triumph came of age as a superbike manufacturer in the late 1990s. The latest specification Daytona 675 has benefited from racing in the Supersport World Championship and revs to a mighty 12,600 rpm redline pumping out 124 bhp.

Above: Named after the famous racetrack in England where Triumph scored many notable victories over the years, the Thruxton 900 evokes memories of the classic cafe racers of an earlier era. The 2010 Special Edition featured a powder-coated red frame and white bodywork.

Right: Triumph's current line-up of cruisers includes the Thunderbird. The standard model is powered by a liquid-cooled 1,600 cc parallel-twin engine, while a big bore variant is also available with an extra 100 cc added to the engine capacity. It is the first belt-driven Triumph since 1922.

Opposite: Triumph's contemporary take on the Bonneville theme evokes the classic styling of the iconic Bonneville that first appeared in 1959. That machine used a 649 cc vertical twin; the 2010 Bonneville has an 865 cc unit that employs modern fuel-injection technology for improved fuel economy.

Above: The Speed Triple was launched by Triumph in 1994. It used an 885 cc triple engine and the same aluminum frame as the 1997 Daytona sportster. The current version is powered by a 675 cc liquid-cooled triple, while the Triple R variant (pictured) adds supersport suspension and brakes.

Opposite: There has never been a production motorcycle like Yamaha's intimidating and brutally powerful V-Max, which was first unveiled back in 1985. The mighty Max remains in the range with its essential personality barely changed, and its reputation for raw power is very much still in place.

Below: The intimidating-looking Yamaha XJR1300 is a pure retro musclebike. It's based around the old upright riding style that requires some serious manhandling through the corners. The engine is a 1,251 cc air-cooled 16-valve in-line four that produces 72 kW (97 bhp) of power at 8,000 rpm.

Above: Yamaha's FZ1 Fazer range debuted in the early 2000s and a second-generation of Fazers with a new chassis and engine launched in 2006. Built around a 998 cc supersport-based engine, for 2010 the ECU mapping has been revised to achieve improved throttle response in low to mid revs.

Right: The MT series from Yamaha has been manufactured since 2005. The MT01 has a powerful 1,670 cc air-cooled overhead-valve V-twin engine mounted in a nimble sports chassis that features sports-derived suspension.

Left: The TDM900 is the latest incarnation of Yamaha's TDM range. This one is billed as an all-rounder, equally at home on the city streets as it is cruising on the open road. The engine is a compact 897 cc fuel-injected parallel twin, and it comes with a long-range fuel tank and luggage rack for touring.

Right: Sharp styling has been a feature of the YZF-R1 ever since Yamaha launched the original model in 1998. The current 998 cc model retains the look, while much of the underlying technology and layout derives from Yamaha's MotoGP-winning M1 racebike.

Fast and Furious

Right: Motocross is a form of motorcycle racing held on enclosed off-road circuits. It traces its origins back to British scrambling competitions. The name is a portmanteau term derived from the words "motorcycle" and "cross-country."

Below: The major motocross series in the United States is the AMA Motocross Championship. Inaugurated in 1972, it is sanctioned by the American Motorcyclist Association.

Above: *Motocross puts incredible demands on the riders, who must keep complete control of a fast-moving and reasonably heavy bike while also maintaining top speed throughout the race and frequently taking to the air in bone-rattling jumps.*

Right: Rain, poor visibility, and muddy conditions are all grist to the mill for any competitor riding in an outdoor-series motocross event. Classes are typically organized according to the sizes of the engines that power the bikes and a race day will generally involve two rounds of competition.

Below: BMW offers three versions of its G650 X-series—the X-Country is a trail bike, a versatile road-going machine with off-road ability, the X-Moto is a supermoto, essentially a motocross machine converted to road use, and the X-Challenge (pictured) is a proper off-road enduro bike.

Above: Alex Salvini is an Italian motocross rider who races for the Husqvarna team in the MX3 class of the FIM-sanctioned Motocross World Championship. In 2009 he was runner-up to World Champion Pierre Renet representing Suzuki.

Above: *Freestyle motocross (FMX) is a relatively new variation of supercross. It does not involve racing; instead the rider concentrates on performing acrobatic stunts while making jumps on his motocross bike. The winner is chosen by judges assessing trick difficulty and aerial style.*

Left: *There are two main types of Freestyle event: Big Air (also known as Best Trick) in which each rider gets two jumps from a dirt-covered ramp, and Freestyle Motocross, where riders perform two routines on a course consisting of multiple jumps of varying lengths and angles.*

Above: A mind-boggling range of moves and tricks have evolved in Freestyle. Riders need great skill and a lot of courage—accidents and injuries are not uncommon.

Right: For many years motocross bikes almost exclusively used two-stroke engines, then Yamaha began to blaze a trail with its four-stroke machines. The YZ450F with its rearward-slanted engine remains a stalwart in the company's line-up.

Below: The nimble YZ250F is the 450F's smaller cousin. The engine is a 250 cc dohc four-stroke single.

Above: The beach resort at Scheveningen, The Hague, in the Netherlands is the venue for the Red Bull Knockout, which bills itself as the toughest motocross beach race in the world. Riders come from around the world to compete while more than 150,000 spectators throng the shore to watch.

Above: The Honda CRF series consists of a line of four-stroke motocross and trail motorcycles that Honda launched in 2002. The current CRF250R uses a 249 cc Unicam engine design—the compact cylinder head incorporates a single cam that opens both the intake and exhaust valves.

Right: Beach racing is an offshoot of enduro and motocross racing. Riders on solo motorcycles, quad bikes, or even sidecar combinations compete on a course marked out on a beach, often with man-made jumps and sand dunes being added to the mix to make the course tougher.

Left: Speedway is a motorcycle sport involving four, or sometimes up to six, riders competing over four counter-clockwise laps of a flat, oval track usually consisting of dirt or loosely packed shale. Speedway motorcycles use only one gear and have no brakes—it's flat out all the way.

Below: Competitors slide their machines sideways on the loose surface of the speedway track, powersliding or broadsiding into the bends. On the straight sections of the track the bikes reach speeds approaching 70 mph (113 kph). Note the dirt deflector fitted alongside the rear wheel of this racer.

Above: The G 450 X is the first BMW enduro bike to be developed for professional competitive racing. The design aims to keep the mass of the machine concentrated as near as possible to the low center of gravity. To this end the 2.2-gallon (8.5-liter) fuel tank is positioned under the rider's seat.

Above: Enduro is a sport that is run mainly off-road, generally in time-trial stages in which competitors race against the clock. Early or late running incurs penalties.

Left: Motorcycle road racing takes a multitude of forms, from top-level Grand Prix events to relatively small meets for local enthusiasts. Races may be run on purpose-built tracks or even on closed public roads, such as at the Isle of Man TT.

Right: Road racing demands concentration, skilled bike control, and courage. There are numerous classes catering for small capacity bikes right through to powerful superbikes.

Opposite: This shows the rugged terrain over which enduro bikes race. The machines are specialized—the long suspension of a motocross bike is combined with features required to make it legal for any public road parts of the course.

Left: *MotoGP is at the pinnacle of motorcycle road racing. It is currently divided into three classes: for 125 cc singles, Moto2 (for 600 cc four-strokes), and MotoGP (for 800 cc four-strokes). The machines are purpose-built and are not available in street-legal road-going versions as Superbikes are.*

Opposite: *Nicky Hayden, aka the Kentucky Kid, is an outstanding American professional motorcycle racer who won the MotoGP World Championship in 2006. He is seen here on the Honda Repsol bike at the Malaysian Grand Prix during the season in which he won the title.*

Below: *Loris Capirossi is a hugely experienced Italian Grand Prix racer with more than 300 starts under his belt. He won the 250 cc world title for Aprilia in 1998. Between 2003 and 2007 he piloted bikes for the Ducati MotoGP team, as shown here, and then switched in 2008 to ride for Suzuki.*

Above: *Smooth and precise—Ducati Marlboro team rider Casey Stoner cornering during testing prior to the 2010 MotoGP season. In 2007 six poles and ten race wins, including three of the first four races, took him storming to his first GP title by an amazing margin of 125 points.*

Right: James Ellison raced for the Yamaha Tech 3 MotoGP team during the 2006 season. He is seen here competing in the F1 Grand Prix at the Sepang International Circuit in Malaysia. In 2007 he switched to the AMA Superbike series in the United States racing for the Corona Honda team.

Above: Preseason testing is an important time for MotoGP teams as they try to set up their race bikes for optimum performance and reliability. Honda Repsol rider Dani Pedrosa is seen here testing in February 2010 wearing the number 26, which he first carried in his 2006 debut season.

Right: American John "Hopper" Hopkins currently races in the Superbike World Championship. He previously competed in MotoGP—in 2002 for the Red Bull Yamaha team. He joined the Suzuki squad a year later, for a five-year spell, and then raced for Kawasaki (as seen here in Spain) in 2008.

Above: American Colin Edwards—or the Texas Tornado—here seen during testing at the Sepang circuit in Malaysia in 2007, is a two-time World Superbike champion for Honda who has competed in MotoGP since 2003. He now rides for the Monster Yamaha Tech 3 independent team.

Right: Italian showman and superstar, Valentino Rossi pulls a wheelie on his Fiat Yamaha at the Malaysian Grand Prix in 2009. Rossi is a phenomenon. He won the World Championship an astonishing seven times between 2001 and 2009, always with the lucky number 46 on his motorcycle.

Index

Picture Credits

a = above, b = below, r = right, l = left, c = center

© Roland Brown: 15al, 16a, 16b; Phil Masters 8b, 9, 17, 18ar, 19, 20, 21r; Oli Tennent 10, 12, 13r, 14, 15ar, 15b, 18al, 18b, 21al.

© shutterstock.com: afaizal 60al, 60bl, 60br, 61, 62cl, 63al; Walter G Arce 1; Anna Chelnokova 53ar; Crok Photography 59al; CTR Photos 52ar; digitalsport-photoagency 62br; Eric Gevaert 56ar, 56b; Andreas Gradin 54l; Khafizov Ivan Harisovich 52bl; Imagemaker 62ar; Jaggat 59br; Marcel Jancovic 57a, 57b; Keith Robinson 59bl; Luiz Rocha 55al; Ljupco Smokovski 4–5; B. Stefanov 52cr, 53al; Filipe B. Varela 54ar; Hemin Xylan 63r.

Motorcycle manufacturers' press pictures:
© Aprilia: 22ar, 22cr, 22bl. © Benelli: 23al, 23bl, 23ar, 23cr. © Boss Hoss Cycles, Inc: 28al, 28ar, 28bl. © Buell: 29br. © BMW AG: 26, 27al, 27ar, 27br, 53br, 58, 59ar. © Cagiva: 30al. © Ducati: 13al, 32, 33bl, 33ar. © Harley-Davidson®: 6–7, 34a, 34b, 35, 36, 37al, 37ar, 37bc, 37br. © Honda Motor Co. Ltd: 38, 39al, 39ar, 39br, 39bc, 56al. © Indian Motorcycle Company: 29al, 29ar. © Kawasaki Motors UK: 2, 40, 41ac, 41ar, 41bl. © MV Agusta: 30ar, 30br, 31. © Suzuki Motor Corporation: 42al, 42bl, 42ar, 43, 44al, 44bl, 44ar, 45. © Triumph Motorcycles Ltd: 46, 47al, 47ar, 47bc, 47br. © Yamaha Motor: 48al, 48bc, 48br, 49, 50l, 50ar, 51al, 51ar, 51b, 55r, 55bl.

Creative Commons License: 33al; El Caganer 8a; Elenchos 33br; Jean-Pol Grandmont 11a; Guilaune 24l; Craig Howell 11b; Jordi Rovira 24ar, 25; selbst 30bl; Peter Shanks 3.

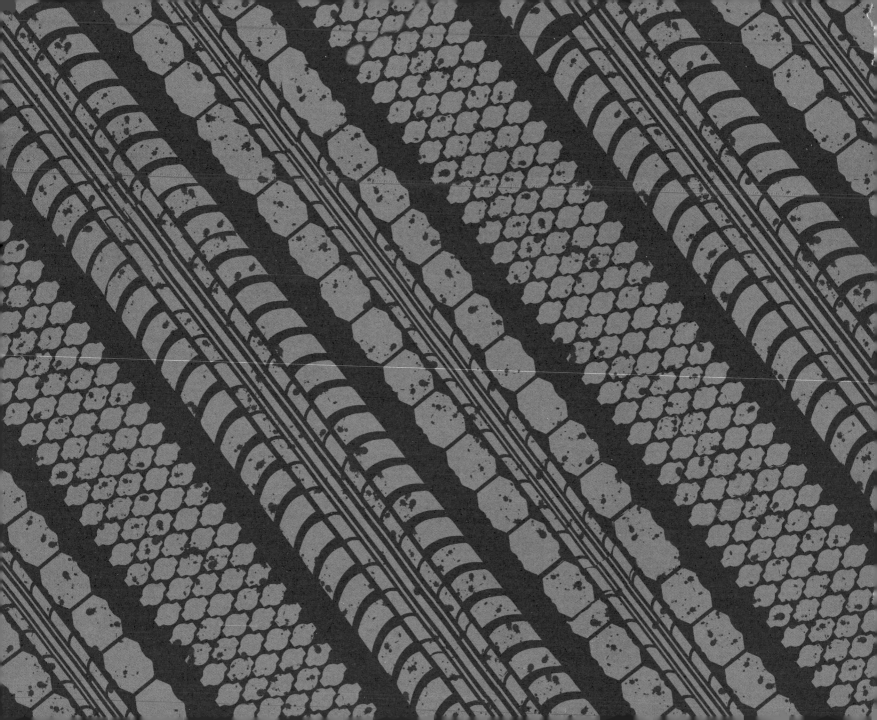